AF345527

Somewhere I talk to the Moon

Samiksha Rungta

Leadstart
INKSTATE

ISBN 978-93-90040-12-4
Copyright © Samiksha Rungta, 2020

First published in India 2021 by Leadstart Inkstate
A Division of One Point Six Technologies Pvt Ltd

Sales Office:
Unit No.25/26, Building No.A/1,
Near Wadala RTO,
Wadala (East), Mumbai – 400037 India
Phone: +91 969933000
Email: info@leadstartcorp.com
www.leadstartcorp.com

All rights reserved. No part of this publication may be reproduced, stored in or introduced into a retrieval system, or transmitted, in any form, or by any means (electronic, mechanical, photocopying, recording or otherwise) without the prior written permission of the publisher. Any person who does any unauthorised act in relation to this publication may be liable to criminal prosecution and civil claims for damages.

Disclaimer: The views expressed in this book are those of the Author and do not pertain to be held by the Publisher.

Editor: Cora Bhatia
Layouts: Kshitij Dhawale

ABOUT THE AUTHOR

Samiksha Rungta is 19 years old and lives in the beautiful city of Ahmedabad, in Gujarat. She lives with her parents, elder sister and younger brother. She is currently a student at the London College of Fashion (UAL) and is aspiring to become a successful Fashion Designer someday. She acquired her ISC certificate after graduating High School from Welham Girls' School in Dehradun.

She loves reading poetry and some of her biggest inspirations are Robert M. Drake and Megha Rao. When she started pursuing art as a hobby and later as a subject, she learnt how it was actually possible to channel emotions onto paper through different mediums. Her interest in art, led her to discover her love for writing in the process of describing her artwork, through small poems or even short prose.

When she is not spending time playing with dogs she writes poetry. She believes that poetry is a way to depict what a person is thinking better than any other art form. Though she loves dancing, listening to music, sketching and painting just as much as she enjoys writing.

'Somewhere I Talk to The Moon' is her debut book of poetry.

ACKNOWLEDGEMENTS

A human being is a sculpture of a million feelings and emotions. Such a person I happen to be. I am someone who is a statue, given life to by the emotions of those who love me, support me and understand me in ways that God made too complex for just anyone.

'Somewhere, I Talk to The Moon', being my debut novel, it deserves to have the purity of holding the names of all these precious people in my life.

The kind of dedication that has gone into this bundle of papers is not just mine, but several other people, who stood next to me to be my coffee buddies, on sleepless nights and close my notebook and pen at 2:00 am.

I want to thank everyone from my family to my friends, who believed I was capable of writing poetry. The first time I wrote a poem, I was going through the most cliché period of my early teenager life. My friends in school and my 'woodpeckers', still believed in the extremely sappy and over romanticized 15 lines that I wrote when, like every other 14-year-old, I had decided that love doesn't exist and it is nonsense. They kept pushing me to fill my notebook with more work, be it short, long, sad or happy. I never heard any of my friends demotivate me, but they sure were my personal editors and advisors on how I should modify my work. They respected the fact that I was not confident about my poems, but also nagged me to put it into places outside of just my notebook or my diary.

So, this is for all of you guys.

Writing poetry about your deepest feelings makes it a little tough to confidently be able to share it with all the people in your life, like family. I had this constant fear of other's opinions about me and what I felt, which kept me from showing my work to anyone else. My family taught me to listen to the opinions of only those who mattered and the rest of the world would just cooperate. So here I am laying my heart bare.

I would like to deeply thank all those who came and left from my life. All those who made me feel a million things in a million different ways, being the push behind each and every poem. I wonder what I would have done had you not made me happy, broken my heart in endless little pieces or picked me up and hugged me to put those pieces together again. You are the real heroes.

Lastly, this novel would not have been a possibility without the opportunity provided to me by the extremely generous team of LEADSTART PUBLISHING. Thanking you from all my heart and a big hug for each one for believing in a teenager's thoughts and aspirations, for providing her with a platform to reach out to other people and most importantly helping her attain the fulfilment of a dream she never thought could actually be fulfilled. Always and forever grateful.

ABOUT THE BOOK

All that you feel is what you are and more.

All that you see is what this world is and more.

But when you see what you feel,

That's when you know who you are.

When the tears from your eyes wet your pillow cover,

you will know the comfort of the hand that will wipe them.

When everything is dark and sad,

you will know the smile that will brighten your day.

When the only thing you remember is the sound of your scream,

you will know the voice that will sing a song for you.

When the only feeling you remember is blue,

you will know the one that will paint you a rainbow.

When you feel that love has been lost,

you will know the touch of the arms that hold you close.

When you want to fall apart and break,

you will know the words that will pick you up,

hold your hand, motivate you to move ahead.

You will know that you're not alone.

SYNOPSIS

Most of the thoughts in our mind, do not know where they come from or where they are going to go next. It is in our hands to channel them in whichever way our heart desires. Some of us turn them into songs, which sing the tears and the smiles in our minds. Some of us begin writing diaries where we know the pages will not judge us, so we lay our heart bare. Then comes the passage of books and poetry. This is the passage chosen by the kind who feel they want to share their tears and smiles for the reason that it would make them feel better and make another soul in the world smile.

Human relation is a strange thing. It is one of the most unpredictable things of all time. They are creatures with so much inside of them that they not know how to handle and go about it, when it all comes pouring out. Co-existence is a very important thing to understand because as much as we hate to admit to it, we do depend on this race and every kind of it.

The question is how much do we actually depend on, how much do we all actually even agree to show?

My poems talk about the deepest things that I am afraid to tell, but not afraid to give as help, as motivation or in any form that would make a difference. All of us have our whims, fantasies and vices that we may not even know of and in forms, which we may never even realize. These poems talk about mine, the ones that I couldn't ignore, the ones that make me who I am.

And hereby I lay my heart and soul bare, with the only hope that it would help another come out of the light and embrace themselves in a different light that they were neglecting all this while. I only hope that these poems give you the motivation to move ahead with a smile because nothing ever looked more beautiful on a human. Your flaws are just a part of you to increase your beauty and only those who deserve to understand this will appreciate you, even when your face is buried in your tears, you will know then who needs to be a part of your journey and who doesn't.

You are not the only one, you are beautiful, you are the best kind of you.

CONTENTS

I.   POEMS

1)	CATASTROPHES	14
2)	IN MEMORY OF YOU	16
3)	WHY	18
4)	MINE	20
5)	ONCE AGAIN	24
6)	MY FRIENDS	26
7)	OBLITERATE	30
8)	DO I?	32
9)	CONSIGN TO OBLIVION	34
10)	RAW	36
11)	THINGS I'LL NEVER SAY OUT LOUD	38
12)	MOROSE	40
13)	WHAT DOES HOPE LOOK LIKE?	44
14)	FIX YOU?	46
15)	FAMILIAR	48
16)	PERSPECTIVE	50
17)	UNADELTERED	52
18)	CRUMBLING	54
19)	CONFRONTATIONAL	56
20)	IN COMPLETE TRUTH	60
21)	BOON OR CURSE?	62
22)	AFFIRMATION	66

23)	REMINISCENCE	70
24)	FORSAKEN	74
25)	TANGENTIAL	78
26)	ELUSIVE	80
27)	ABSTINENT	82
28)	THE BETRAYAL	84
29)	EVOCATIVE	86
30)	THE GLOAMING	88
31)	PERTURBATION	90
32)	LAUDATORY	92
33)	SINFUL	94
34)	HUES	98
35)	THE HALT	100
36)	TRULY BESOTTED	102
37)	ADIEU	104
38)	IMMISCIBLE	106
39)	2:00 AM THOUGHTS	108
40)	AXIOM	110
41)	PLENTEOUS	114
42)	ENSHRINED	116
43)	FAILED ATTEMPTS	120
44)	COME BACK?	122
45)	COMPLYING	124
46)	ANTICIPATING	128
47)	RAINBOW	132
48)	DETACHMENT	136
49)	EUPHORIA	140

50) CONFESSED FEELINGS   144

51) BEAUTY   148

52) IS IT REALLY OVER?   150

53) IS IT TOO MUCH?   154

54) BARE HONESTY   158

55) TRANQUILITY   162

56) ARE YOU TALKING TO ME?   166

57) IF I LOVE YOU   170

58) I SHOULD HAVE KNOWN   174

59) IS THIS LIVING?   178

II. SO LITTLE YET SO MUCH

1) BLISS   182

2) MINUTIAE   184

3) YEARNING   186

4) FONDNESS   188

5) CHARADE   190

6) REMEMBRANCE   192

7) HOME   194

8) USUAL   196

9) ALIEN   198

10) ADMIRATION   200

11) TRIUMPH   202

12) ASTONISHING   204

13) CONCERN   206

14) INTIMACY   208

I. POEMS

Catastrophes

There is this thing about tornadoes,

how they leave my hair

in a complete mess.

There is this thing about whirlwinds,

how they leave my head

spinning in circles.

There is this thing about tsunamis,

how it takes them a minute

to destroy everything.

I wonder,

which one does it better.

Them or you?

Photo Credit: Anonymous

In memory of you

Your laughter echoes.

It's louder than the rap music my friends are blaring

in the room outside.

I get lost in us,

in our past, till I feel the burn in my throat,

once again.

My guilt is reaching up,

all the way to my head.

Another thought of suicide rings the doorbell of my mind.

I welcome it with a smile as I open the door,

and cookies maybe?

Another burning sensation in my throat.

This time it is not the guilt.

And suddenly everything goes black.

Photo Credit: Samiksha Rungta

Why?

My eyes burn.

The tears down my cheeks are heavy, it hurts.

A lot more than I thought.

I should not have cried.

It hurt holding it in, but that pain was bearable.

Each tear is a sign that I gave up.

Each tear broke the wall that I had almost completed building.

Then why shall I now let it fall?

Why do the bricks and the cement so easily melt away by this salty drop of water?

I don't understand.

My mind is in a frenzy of emotions, hatred.

Towards myself and everything else.

I can sense the negativity in abundance.

It is bad for health.

But,

So were you.

Photo Credit: Dipesh Kundnani

Mine

By the day, it is getting tougher to breathe.

I'm running out of time.

The windows in my room remain shut,

so do the blinds.

It is getting harder to gasp for air.

Can I help it?

I have been trying, trust me.

I am not trying to give up, but I don't care anymore,

If I live or not.

You ask me why my eyes are bloodshot.

You are scared if you are the reason.

Aren't you?

The dream catcher stopped helping years ago.

Nightmares are the only ones I associate with anymore.

At least they aren't feeding me lies!

I am tired of smiling and keeping the truth hidden,

and veiled always.

You have read my poems.

There was always more to them than them just being beautiful.

I kept telling you.

I gave enough away for you to realize the storm

building within me.

That is the universal problem you see,

'ignorance is bliss'.

Well, are you ready to bear the consequence of that phrase?

 Are you strong enough to?

When you found those pills,

you yelled your lungs out at me.

Did you ever wonder why I even had them with me, in the first
place?

You stopped listening to me, a long time ago,

Everyone did, eventually.

Don't wonder why this paper is blotchy, it isn't my tears,

not at all.

I am awake, nights and nights,

ever wondered why?

How would you know?

I never showed it, I never will.

I am scared to take another breath,

it chokes me the second I try.

It will already be the next morning, when you read this.

Don't come looking for me,

I couldn't find myself either.

There isn't a chance of you succeeding at it.

I am hurting, I had been for a while.

I cannot talk about it to anyone.

No one is going to get it,

No one ever did,

No one ever will.

Photo Credit: Samiksha Rungta

Once again

For the thousandth time, I felt as if I was trying too hard.

I wanted to understand that it is an endless cycle,

Where I continue trying in a helpless manner

And you pretend to not see it,

even after seeing it.

I feel that someday I will reach that point, where you

will understand the worth of all my trying, failed attempts.

Someday, you will realize that maybe

you should have respected it, just a little.

I believe that one day instead of me,

you will try to convince me, otherwise.

But then once again, I try to make myself believe

That this day will come.

I try, yet again.

Photo Credit: Vedant Jain

My friends

Addiction, she thought, was a wrong word to use.

Those white substances, she subsumed them.

After all, they were her best friends,

Or so she believed.

They took her to a juncture, where her mind and soul were one.

She became a henchman to those powders;

which were alien to her, just a few months ago.

She said the world around her, which stopped her,

was an adversary.

No one understood her actions.

She said it was an additive to her grace, her poise.

Though she knew her British beauty drowned away a little
more

With each puff that she released.

It was an excuse for her.

She said it was to chasten herself, chasten her soul,

for everything she had let it go through.

The sober mind felt like German to her.

All that her vocabulary recognized was hemp, heroine, cannabis and ecstasy.

Who would have believed she was the editor-in-chief of her school's paper.

The state of dilemma they created,

Was where she desired to be.

She craved for the delusional world they portrayed.

And

each time she inhaled

she thought,

"Is that what they say happens to people with a rough childhood?"

Photo Credit: Dipesh Kundnani

Obliterate

The first time I saw you; you were reading a Sylvia Plath

and I remember thinking, 'he has to be a nerd'.

The last time I kissed you,

I remember thinking, how to tell you that your cologne was the best,

even though, just ten minutes back, I had fought with you to buy one of my choice.

The first time you held my hand,

I wanted to tell you that it's the only time I felt as if my broken pieces were together.

The last time I looked into your eyes as we said goodbye,

I felt the cool breeze take away every ounce of respect that I had left in my body for you.

Ever since, I keep forgetting.

I keep forgetting what it felt like to be in love.

 What it felt like to be a part of someone.

What it feels like to be happy only by sharing a milkshake with someone.

I keep forgetting everything.

Everything but the time when you had held my hands in front of everyone

and told me that this would last forever.

I remember.

Photo Credit: Anonymous

Do I?

I want to live.

I don't want to live, rather I'm scared.

My depression is picking pace.

 I left it in another city, but it seems like it caught up.

It always does and yet I always let it go,

instead of destroying it right where it is.

I don't want to destroy it either.

I wonder what all it knows about me,

parts and secrets about me, which aren't known to me.

Is it safe to unleash that part?

Is it safe to show those parts of me, which it keeps buried in its intimate darkness?

I don't care anymore.

It almost seems like I'm dying without the knowledge of those parts.

I wonder what those parts hold, which is making the depression hold me hostage.

I wonder why they hold so much importance to me.

I'm ready to be bound to this strange black hole just to reach out to them.

It has got to be something of great value, which my depression holds against me.

Sometimes, I wonder.

I wonder, I hope it isn't you it's got?

Sometimes, I believe.

I know it's you.

No wonder I'm betting my life on it.

Photo Credit: Dipesh Kundnani

Consign to oblivion

I keep forgetting things.

My untied shoelaces,

My lunch time,

My sleep schedule.

I keep forgetting names.

My driver,

The lady who washes my clothes,

The uncle on the chai stall, near my house.

I keep forgetting feelings.

The first time I came home from boarding school,

My first kiss,

The first time I got cat called,

The first time I held my little brother.

I keep forgetting.

How to live.

Photo Credit: Dipesh Kundnani

Raw

It was 2:56 am. I was lying in bed.

I was reading an Instagram post that said,

"Someone is going to cry. It's probably going to be me."

Randomly, my eyes start watering. Both of them.

I didn't even think of anything sad.

I thought it's just my body.

It can't take any more of the nonsense that I keep stacking up inside it.

It's just its way of making me realize that it needs to clean up.

I ignore it. Another tear falls.

Now, it's getting strange.

I go to your profile, see your pictures.

I recall.

The waterworks increase.

I give my body another slap on its face by stacking up more nonsense by the minute.

More tears.

Another try by my body to cleanse.

I waste the attempt, yet again.

Photo Credit: Dipesh Kundnani

Things I'll never say out loud

How much I wanted you to stay the night of the homecoming dance.

I wished I could have met you one last time, without crying, when I saw you in that hospital gown.

I wish I missed the flight that day to stay for the concert.

My mind is a dark abyss that you shouldn't come near.

I cry myself to sleep because reality tells me to do so.

I cannot choose between chocolate and caramel.

I'm scared to fall in love because I will stop believing in it, just as fast as I fall out of it.

It's going to be okay.

Photo Credit: Anonymous

Morose

Sleep has become a guest,

just like my uncle, who visits a few times.

I told him that I like the chocolates that he gets me.

So, he gets them each time he comes over.

My sleep learnt that I liked thoughts of you,

So, for the brief time that it comes over, it gets them along.

The cycles begin.

No sleep. Thoughts of you.

What next?

No sleep.

No thoughts of you.

Tears. Stained pillow covers.

Not caused by the lack of thoughts of you.

Not caused by the lack of sleep.

What next?

No sleep.

Enter depression.

No thoughts of you still.

Tears.

Blood stained pillow covers.

More tears.

Yelling, screaming, the insides of my mind exploding.

Blood stained bed covers.

Short hair that I hate, plus red highlights I had never imagined.

Successfully transformed.

What next?

I don't know.

Who are you? What are tears?

What is sleep?

Who am I?

Only piece of memory left,

Thoughts of you.

No sleep.

Cycle ends.

Photo Credit: Dipesh Kundnani

What does hope look like?

It looks like the petite brown puppy that was just born.

It looks like the sparkle in her eyes each time she sees him.

It looks like the tear that falls from the mother's eyes,

on meeting her children after a year.

It looks like the bouquet of fresh roses he still keeps on her empty side, every anniversary.

It looks like the medicine that is fed to him every morning, at the rehab.

It looks like an episode of Game of Thrones to distract her,

when she comes home crying after a breakup.

It looks like the lantern the young boy in the slum nearby lights every night,

to secretly read a school textbook.

It looks like the photo frame of a picture of their marriage that she dusts every day.

It looks like the heartbeat of a suicide attempt patient on the monitor.

It looks like the smile that she carries every day.

Photo Credit: Vedant Jain

Fix You

A life free of conflict is a life that hasn't been lived.

It's the drive, it's the push.

So if you push it away, what will drive you ahead?

Some say it drives them crazy,

but today, how do you achieve anything until crazy has touched it.

I don't think we're getting anywhere,

with all the crying and cribbing about things going wrong.

If they don't go wrong,

how do you ever make something right?

It has to be a situation that annoys you that troubles you.

Only then will you feel like getting rid of the trouble.

Let this get to you.

Let it push you to the edge,

and pull yourself up right at the point,

when you are dangling and a millisecond

away from falling off the edge.

Let the crazy get inside your head and take it over.

Let it keep repeating constantly that you are nothing.

You will thank it one day.

One day, you will call this crazy your best friend.

It's what pushed you through, even though, it drove you a little crazy.

Let this crazy fix you.

Photo Credit: Vedant Jain

Familiar

I need something to hold on to.

While I sleep, that is, of course.

A childhood habit you can say.

I have a side pillow that I clutch on to,

when I drift into dreamland.

When I wake up in the morning,

it's usually on the floor.

Why do I throw it off the bed?

Do I do it intentionally or,

is it just an unconscious action?

I do not know.

But it's not by my side when I wake every morning,

the way it was the night before.

Doesn't it remind you of you?

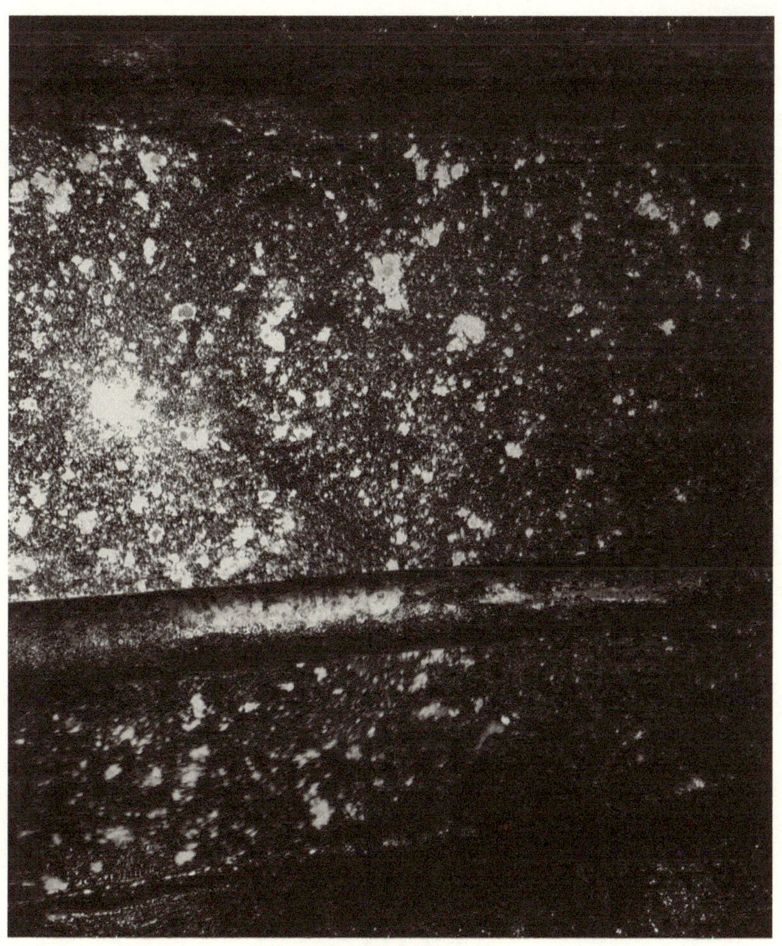

Photo Credit: Vedant Jain

Perspective

You strive to be so close to someone,

in the midst of the underlying ghost of thought that's telling you,

to stay away from them.

You want to run to them and give them a hug,

because they don't deserve to be treated the way they are being treated right now.

You want to tell them that time doesn't change,

how much you can ever care about a person,

Time and feelings aren't friends.

However long it's been,

I will still feel the same concern as always,

The worst part is there is nothing I can do about it.

There is nothing I can change,

to make you believe that nothing has changed.

There is nothing I can do,

to make you love you like I do.

Photo Credit: Vedant Jain

Unadulterated

Sometimes, I wish we looked at things,

with a touch of mud and not of glitter.

Sometimes, I wish we saw

that the sky is usually more grey than white.

Sometimes, I wish boys liked girls,

who are a lazy Sunday morning and not a Saturday night.

Sometimes, I wish we spent more time,

in the fields than a cafe.

Sometimes, I wish to write you

an ink-blotched letter with a feather, not an email.

Sometimes, just sometimes,

I wish things were more real.

Photo Credit: Dipesh Kundnani

Crumbling

I am caught up in this web called life.

The web is hanging above a valley,

one side of which is love and the other one, lust.

Some of them will say that love overpowers lust...

then why are there still more rape cases than marriage ceremonies?

Then there are some who say lust overpowers love,

then why are there people trying so hard to maintain their relationships

over the seas, instead of indulging in multiple one-night-stands?

The web weighs me down more and more,

getting further entangled in it, because I realize

that my life would never be a complete combination of love and lust.

The influence that the two have on me,

can never be profoundly balanced.

Then there is this thing called 'hope' at the bottom of the valley that I want to reach, even if it's takes the web breaking and my soul crushing.

I am not afraid of hurting,

because how do u crush something that is already so destroyed.

Photo Credit: Dipesh Kundnani

Confrontational

Hey brother!

How are you? We talked ten minutes ago, but then why do I still ask?

I ask you this, because I don't remember you.

You are like a silhouette in my life that will always be there,

I'm not sure if always 'for me'.

I don't remember the last time you said to me,

"Hey! How is school going on? I am sure you aced your exams!"

 Or even, "Stupid, you cannot do art! I am better at it!"

Ever since the day the words, "You are a fucking bitch," left your mouth,

I knew I had misjudged your priorities.

Well, I was right, wasn't I?

I tried to warn you but you said, "You don't understand anything! She is 'the one' for me!"

Well, I guess your apparent priority isn't even a part of you anymore,

ever since you walked in on her cheating.

Brother, I never wanted anything bad for you,

but all you gave me back was worse.

And today without any shame I ask you, "What were you thinking that day?"

Love,

A lost relation.

Photo Credit: Dipesh Kundnani

In complete truth

"He is so hot," I tell my sister,

"I think, he is the one."

I'm not exactly the mind reader kinds,

but I know that she's thinking,

"She's 18 and she will fall for every other guy,

until she realizes who is her 'the one' one day."

Too embarrassed to say it out loud,

I quietly let my mind tell hers,

"No, I'm serious about this.

Never before today have I ever wanted to

paint the walls of 'my' own house with someone."

Photo Credit: Anonymous

Boon or curse?

Is overthinking choking me?

Or the strange being in my lungs, growing by the day,

feeding on my soul.

I reach out for air, but the night is too still, it seems.

Is it the same hospital gown I see or the monotonous shades of
blue

that rule over my not so callous,

but exceedingly depressive mind?

It has got a decimating effect. I'm quite familiar with it.

The doctor declaims,

"People always leave. This ewer that is cancer, drowns them
all."

The fear of euthanasia enfolds me,

 Till the sudden feel of my mother's tear on my lips, snaps me
out of it.

The needles that inject and know the many parts of my body,

provide a strange euphoria of getting away with this entirety,
commonly called 'the world'.

The Holy Cross on the wall, of the melancholic hospital room, tilts.

There must be a thunderstorm outside,

Or so I wanted to believe.

The camaraderie of the glucose tube and the back of my hand,

was the only understandable thing remaining.

My consciousness is snatched away by the nurse,

providing me with the numbness that I had longed for.

My mind goes blank, turns into a black hole.

I am reunited with my best mate – insomnia.

My cagey voice echoes in my head, 'It hurts ma!'

When I had coughed out blood, for several nights that came and went.

When that prestigious day arrived,

demise and worry replaced the air around me.

I was breathing in fear, not oxygen.

I was ready to get the strange being out of my dying lungs, or was I?

"Half an hour and you will be okay!"

He said with a smile, whose confidence everyone else saw, underlying worry I saw.

In that moment, of my mind and heart fighting, in utter

dilemma and confusion;

I glanced at the not so tilted cross.

I sent a silent prayer,

a wish that this judgmental world would not have considered

wise for a fifteen-year-old.

Photo Credit: Grace Fu

Affirmation

The other day, I heard this couple fighting,

  The woman screamed at her significant other, and said,

"Shut the fuck up. All you are is a womanizer."

Then she held her son by the shoulder and said,

"Tom come, I can't let you be in his sight anymore."

She walked away crying.

The man hung his head down in shame.

All I could think of after that was the way the son turned around,

And looked at his dad with utter disgust and yelled,

"If you like other women more than mommy,

  then you can go and like some other boy also, more than me."

  Then he turned to his mom and mouthed a 'sorry for this mom, but I have to do this.'

He looked back at his dad, with fiery eyes.

He picked up his middle finger and screamed,

"You are a worthless dick."

The mom looked at her 13-year-old son,

with pupils dilated out of shock and then smiled at him,

with so much pride that I literally felt it through me.

That day I felt for that boy, but what he said to his dad,

I wanted to repeat to myself day and night, every second, and I did.

I am sorry mom, I didn't know I would turn out like dad.

I couldn't deal with the fact that I became a monster too.

I am sorry I am doing this to you, but it is the only way out and it is the only way I can let u live happily.

I don't want u to suffer again, this time not because of hurt,

but because of all the shame that you will have to go through because of me.

I am sorry mom, but I swear I am doing you a favor.

I love you mom, but I don't deserve you.

Your son,

Tom.

Photo Credit: Anonymous

Reminiscence

They walked into the bar.

It was almost telepathic how I instantly spun around in my seat.

My eyes met hers and however unfortunate I thought for it to be, she recognized me.

My blind date was confused, as I turned back to him, watching them walk towards us,

trying my best to show that what I just witnessed,

didn't kill me a thousand times already.

His hand found my shoulder and without hesitation, I recognized his touch.

I blinked twice, asked my tears to wait for some time,

told my fake smile that she can show herself now and turned towards them.

She hugged me and he gave me an awkward smile,

as though I wasn't even worthy of being a stranger to him.

I was seeing him after six months,

but my heart didn't need even six seconds to fall for that smile,

all over again, just like the old times.

It was clear from the excitement in her eyes

that he had mentioned me as a friend to her and nothing else.

I don't blame him though.

So, what if we had loved each other,

we knew very well we weren't meant to be.

She had seen all our pictures, only the sane ones though.

The ones that shouted, WE ARE JUST ACQUAINTANCES.

Sometimes, I wonder would she have been with him had she seen the ones

that cried and whimpered, I DO LOVE YOU REALLY.

Our love was a flame that burnt bright, but I guess after a while,

he just didn't bother to feed it any more oil.

Our love was one that could cross great oceans, but I guess after a while,

he just decided to swim in the shallow waters.

It wasn't just him; it was me too.

Instead of trying to pull each other out of this tornado,

we lost one another in it.

Photo Credit: Dipesh Kundnani

Forsaken

I think of the coffee table in the cafe next to our apartment.

I'm sitting on it and listening to Pompeii.

The sound of Bastille is spilling out of my earphones,

and suddenly a stranger

walks up to my table and asks me to lower the volume.

I look at you and I can't help but smile, when I think how

you listen to that song on repeat even today in the shower.

When I visited my aunt last week,

she showed me a photo frame that she has kept in her
bedroom.

It's a picture of you, me, her and Marlo, the only dog you've
ever liked.

I remember you asked her where you could buy a dog that
beautiful.

When we did, you named him Marlo.

The lady at my salon was a friend from school.

Do you remember how surprised she was?

when I took you to her and showed her my wedding ring?

She said she would have loved to do my hair at our wedding.

You had joked that you would have wanted yours done too.

The ice cream man has become very old now.

He still remembers how we used to annoy him,

when we couldn't decide which flavor to buy.

He asks about you when I visit alone these days,

without any confusion as to what I should choose.

I tell him you are at the bar just down the road,

not confused about what to have as well.

He gives me a sympathetic smile.

My uncle died yesterday and I went for his funeral. You came
along too.

I told you to dress well and make a neat beard, but as always
you did not listen.

Mother was angry with me for the way you showed up.

"He had a late night at work last night, he was very tired."

She believed the lie, as easily as I believed myself.

You come home from work each night.

Some days early, some days early in the morning.

I say nothing to you as I sleep alone in the bedroom, my pillow
case half wet.

You don't notice. I wish you would.

When I push my blanket aside from on top of me in the middle of the night

to get out of bed and walk around the room,

because my anxiety wouldn't let me sleep,

I want you to hold my hand and pull me back into bed, right inside your blanket,

till where your breath is reaching, wrap your arms around me,

only for the simple reason that you cannot sleep without holding 'your' pillow.

I think about the good old days.

I think about the time when you used to come home on time,

and get me different flowers, every day, so that I wouldn't get bored of any.

I think about the time when I didn't have to wake up in the middle of the night,

because anxiety was an alien feeling to me.

I think about the time when you used to hold me tight each night,

and I would be so enveloped in your love that I didn't notice

the tighter you held me, the more your love escaped into mine,

till there was no more of it left in you.

Photo Credit: Anonymous

Tangential

The past year was like bliss,

felt so good to be in love.

Guess I thought too soon for myself,

And the worst was yet to come.

As I sit on my bedside,

thinking about those wonderous illusions,

a small laugh escapes my lips; it sure was a hasty decision.

My heart aches immensely on feeling the loss of you,

my thoughts wander off into the deepening darkness of
solitude.

The feeling of regret hits me each time you cross my mind,

the happiness that you took away with yourself,

is going to be hard to find.

Thinking about all your promises, a shiver runs down my body,

just amuses me on thinking how you broke them so smoothly.

Everything we had together left scars all over my heart,

with my blood and tears, you created this piece of art.

I tried calling you up the other day,

When you screamed and pushed me off.

My best friend called you names, which didn't affect you at all.

Now, as I lay on the floor,

putting my heart down on this empty sheet,

this letter is to tell you my love,

that I am done dancing to your beat.

A heartless young man or whom I 'liked' to call my boy,

I hope you understand my loud silence,

because it's my heart not a toy.

Photo Credit: Anonymous

Elusive

As I enter the club amongst the crowd,

she stands out, unique and utterly beautiful.

Her little black dress looks a little,

unusual to my eyes.

Her hoodie-with-shorts look, flashes through my mind.

Suddenly, she is encased in a loving kiss,

the only difference that, this time it's not me.

The way she looks at him,

eats me on the inside.

But I think it's time for me to realize that I was the one,

Who played the fool and let her go.

I am the one who destroyed her,

Bubbly, cheeky, innocent soul.

And turned her into this girl I never knew.

A stranger to my heart and my eyes.

Photo Credit: Samiksha Rungta

Abstinent

We stood there like two cartoons,

Who had grown out of being animated.

Looking at the spaceship that we

couldn't quite land.

The glimmering nothingness;

The beautiful darkness;

Calling to us, as they shivered

those stars, in the distance.

Photo Credit: Vedant Jain

The Betrayal

Suddenly, I felt a burning sensation on my cheek.

His hand was rough and harsh.

I woke up startled, drenched in sweat.

I held onto him tight, never realizing

that I was hugging nothing but a lifeless dummy.

Soon after, he left me, but his words

are still etched in my heart,

"Wake up princess. This isn't wonderland.

Learn to face the real world."

I asked him, "When was I ever in wonderland?

You treated me like a rag anyway."

He said, "Don't look at the situation this way,

That 'I' treated you like a rag.

Look at it this way, 'You let me!' "

Photo Credit: Grace Fu

Evocative

What is my life all about?

It is about her power and her energy

that surrounds me.

It is about her love and affection

that holds me.

It is about her youth and enthusiasm

that ensures me.

It is about her presence and soul

that I cannot feel anymore.

Photo Credit: Dipesh Kundnani

The gloaming

As we tiptoed our way,

through misleading paths,

through the gloomy darkness

of an overwhelming night,

my tear stained eyes

looked at your bloodshot ones, and whispered,

"The silence deafens every atom of mine,

Even more than the gunshots did."

They beckon yours to speak with a longing look.

Yours then say to mine,

"In this same silence, I had called to you my love.

But you walked away. Away from me.

Holding his hands, towards your own destruction."

Photo Credit: Anonymous

Perturbation

When he left me,

he took a piece of my heart along with him.

I felt like I had a hole in me.

My emotions all pouring out from there.

But then you came by; you completed me.

I felt like I was whole again.

You made my soul come alive.

The spark in me began burning again.

And just then, my alarm went off.

I woke up with reality pushing itself in my face.

And then I realized how

just a small, simple thing like reality

can totally, completely ruin your life.

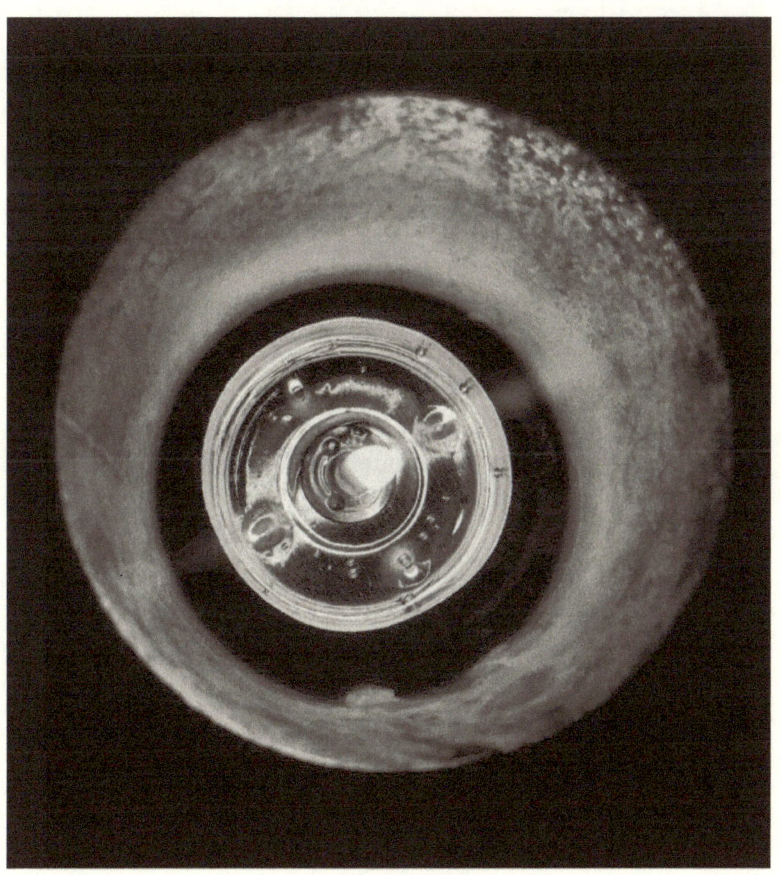

Photo Credit: Vedant Jain

Laudatory

You and me

are two pieces of a puzzle that fit together perfectly.

You and me

are like a lock to a key.

You're everything I need and more.

You're my light at the end of the tunnel.

You're my favorite 'hello' and toughest 'goodbye'.

You're my shadow, the one

who is always by my side.

You're the smile that covers my face,

each time I'm happy.

You're my one and only anchor.

You and I are the perfect two,

and I promise I'd bet my life for you.

Photo Credit: Anonymous

Sinful

Cheated, neglected.

It's not the first time.

Gave up on everything, till you got back the light.

An innocent heart, born in a rich man's manor!

So beautiful and petite, with an adorable demeanor.

How like a princess,

she led her beautiful life.

By her beauty everyone around was completely mesmerized.

One day on a dark night, as fate had it for her

that fragile flower was burned and tattered.

How she was treated like

A shard of glass or some experiment.

Those devils they ruined her for their own amusement.

She did not give up.

She fought for her right.

Had heard God is always around you,

Well 'he' proved the point.

How like a charming prince,

With an armor of dauntless, he saved his angel,

From those ruthless devils.

My angel, he tells her,

No one can ever hurt you.

In my safe haven,

I swear to always protect you.

She tells him softly,

You brought me back to life.

You taught me about the world which is

No better than a sinful knife.

Photo Credit: Anonymous

Hues

On this blank paper, love,

My soul sketched you.

It was etched in the paper;

as my thoughts filled it in with colors,

so vibrant.

It was a true beauty to see

That work of art.

Till my heart, spilled itself on it.

And soon that paper,

was all black.

As though one touch of my heart,

had turned it straight to ashes.

Photo Credit: Vedant Jain

The halt

"Can you hear them my sweet angel?

The melodious sounds from above.

Calling out to you,

To be impinging on the world;

To never back down?"

Today, I grieve on remembering,

My mother's beautiful words.

And I send a silent prayer to her,

"Sorry mum! I couldn't do it.

I didn't stand up to your expectations.

I sold myself to the devil, I let him wear me down.

But I cannot take it anymore. Those memories they irk me.

They are drowning me inside out.

He jostled me into the pits of remorse.

I'm falling hard and fast.

And I just cannot seem to stop myself."

Photo Credit: Dipesh Kundnani

Truly Besotted

I stepped onto the street in the pouring rain.

The water slid straight off my skin.

Washing away with it, scars that were left by him.

I watched the water 'fizzle' on my sinful skin,

Which had become so, due to the things he did covertly,

Things that were not exposed to the world.

I was so busy in thought as to how easily

He turned me from a flamboyant to a lifeless woman.

I was lost so deep, thinking of myself as

Nothing but a very cretinous woman.

I didn't notice the screech of the skidding car.

I was on the ground all of a sudden.

My mind, body, soul all numb.

Just as I was about to sell myself to the heavens above,

My dreamy, blurry vision caught a glimpse of the man in the car.

That sight gnawed at my soul,

Till at one point, I could feel it no more.

Photo Credit: Vedant Jain

Adieu

I used to be so happy, but without you, I'm lost.

In this ocean of people, not knowing who to trust.

My heart aches, each time it beats.

I wonder if you feel that way for me.

I've been sleeping with your sweater,

For the past few nights.

I wonder if you,

Do the same with mine.

It's killing me to get you out of my head.

But I have to because

You've probably found someone new for your bed.

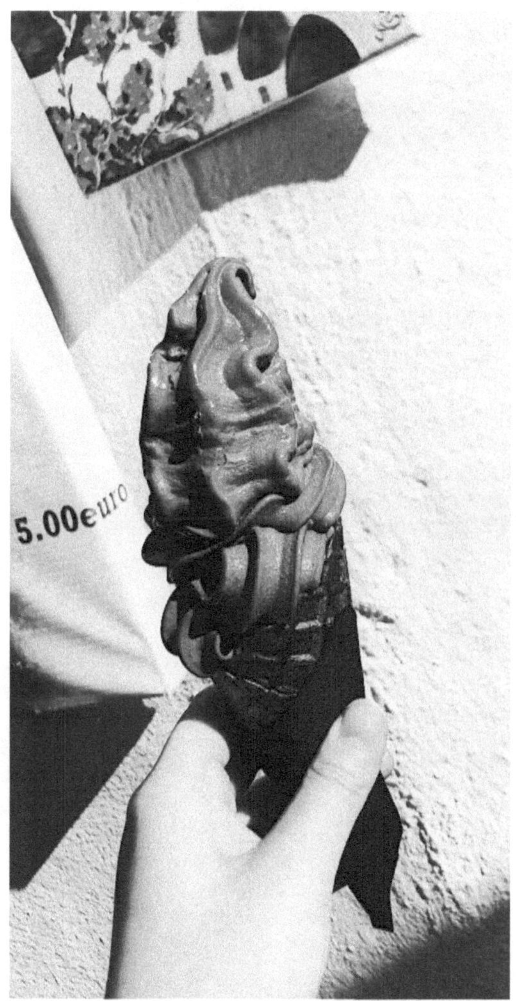

Photo Credit: Grace Fu

Immiscible

The broken spaceship;

The wilted rose;

The soberness of the whiskey glass;

They all play our part.

Two halves of a heart;

Two poles so similar;

That couldn't be kept apart.

Photo Credit: Dipesh Kundnani

2:00 AM Thoughts

How lost do you exactly feel when everything in life,

just comes falling down, all at once?

How exactly do you cope with it?

Like you are in the middle of these smoky woods,

with big trees that have branches longer than rivers that you have seen,

on a moonless night and there's no path anywhere nearby.

The tears fall on the paper, the floor, the rug.

They have been a lot of places.

How much can you bottle up inside yourself?

It will come out one day and that's the best thing to do.

Then why does it make you feel weak? There isn't anyone left around.

Fights with friends who meant the extreme most,

love that has been long lost gone,

family that is so broken you have lost hope if it will ever get fine,

and you yourself.

The tears roll down the cheeks,

leaving trails of the path that should be followed,

but eventually they too disappear.

Where to go now?

Photo Credit: Dipesh Kundnani

Axiom

Dear lover turned cheater,

I don't know why I'm wasting time writing this to you,

But I wasted enough those years, already, so this isn't anything.

I gave you everything you ever asked for.

I gave you my heart, my soul, my skin, my deepest secrets.

I gave you my assurance; I gave you my support and most importantly,

I gave you my love, all of it.

I stood by you, when the world told you that you were wrong.

I lifted up your spirit, when you felt that you were nothing,

when I knew that the reason I was alive today was you.

I fought with my own to show to them,

that you were more than your bike, leather jackets and your bohemian cigars.

I showed you the light you had inside you, which was dimming because you were never ready to believe in it.

What did you give me in return?

A kiss to a woman that was prettier than me.

An 'I love you' to a woman that wore skimpier clothes than me.

Worst of all, you gave all of yourself to someone,

who told you how to talk, how to dress and how to behave because,

she couldn't accept the beauty that you were,

because she didn't like you the way you were,

because she will never see what I saw in you.

– your lover

Photo Credit: Anonymous

Plenteous?

My mind randomly wanders off, sometimes.

To my photo vault.

It reminds me of the good times.

I relive my happiness in it.

I remember that there was a time in my life,

Where I thought of something else, apart from just black.

I look at it to experience the solace,

I once felt when those pictures were still alive.

I look at the photographs that fed me an additive,

which made me forget how my life is falling apart, at the very moment.

I revisit it quite often these days, but I wonder why.

I see and remember.

There once existed a time, where I actually knew how to be happy.

Photo Credit: Vedant Jain

Enshrined

This one is for you and me, because you got me so lovestruck.

As I miss you each day even more,

I look at the sky and all I can think is that

Even though miles apart, we lay under the same one.

Your flaws seem perfect to my eyes that adore them,

Longing to see you more and more each day.

Alive is what I feel, when you hold me tight.

So make this fading moment, fade into infinity.

The stars align, so do heaven and hell,

When you are with me.

I want you here with me forever,

When time freezes this perfect moment.

A simple smile on your face, brightens my soul;

The way a bright star does a gloomy night!

Leave me if you must,

But let me hold you just for a little longer, right now.

Tell me that your arms will ease the pain.

You're my saving grace and

I swear to catch every tear that drops from your eyes.

Kiss me if you must before the lights go out.

I search all through the crowd,

Yours is the only face I see.

Each day it gets better, as we take another step together.

My heart tells me to believe that we were meant to be.

Our rendezvous are where we live out all our dreams.

Infinity is the place till where my love stretches for you.

And I want all the strings attached,

Because you got my heart captured by yours.

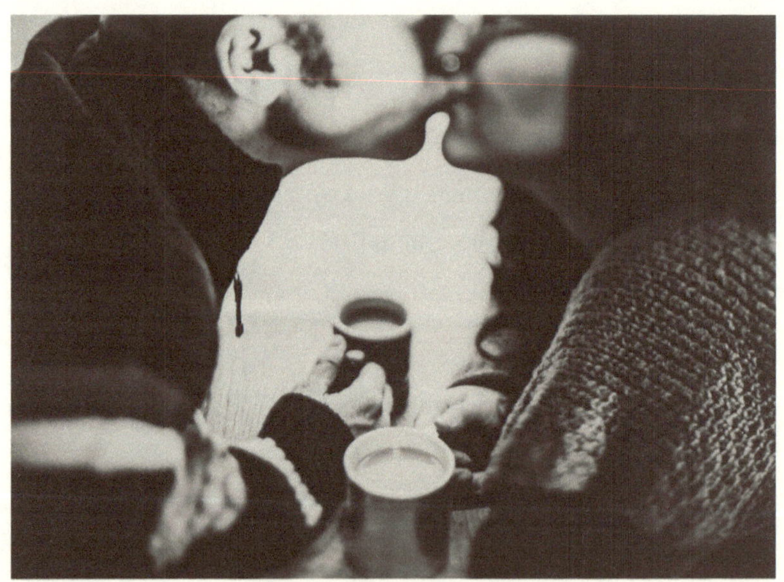

Photo Credit: Anonymous

Failed Attempts

I tried to fix what I had lost with you.

I knew I would be able to,

everyone said I was a fighter.

I wanted to tell you how dark it had become,

since you walked out.

Not just of my heart, but my entire life itself.

I wanted to tell you that I had been living my life,

ever since, for the both of us.

I tried to talk to you, more than once, way more.

I was always told that I could fix this.

I knew I could.

That day, I gave up.

It was new.

An alien feeling.

Photo Credit: Vedant Jain

Come Back?

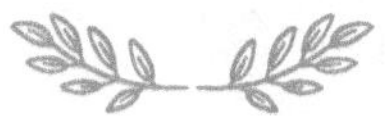

I miss you so much, I know you know it.

Please come back to me,

What have I done to deserve this?

A little chubby kid, with eyes so blue,

The ocean adores them, the sky does too.

When I was three I remember,

As we walked down the road;

It was a dark cloudy night,

But I loved it, because I was with you.

I remember when you taught me,

How to cycle down the road.

I scraped my knee a lot of times,

But you showed me how to be strong.

When we went camping,

The wild dogs, they scared me.

To protect me, you fought them,

Without hearing a word from me.

You had been my role model,

Ever since I came into this world.

You never let me miss mom,

Or at any time feel her loss.

As I turn 15 today,

I send a silent prayer to you dad.

Please come back, I need you,

My hero, my superman.

Photo Credit: Grace Fu

Complying

These x-ray eyes scan me from head to toe.

My lacy underwear is only

Till where their vision stretches.

Nothing for feelings and skin beneath.

Our blurred visages hide,

The undeniable underlying emotional factor.

Express; a word that sounds good when spoken,

When implemented, to express our tear-stained thoughts,

Only get to hear,

'She will cry, she is a girl after all.'

Through ears that bleed due to these harsh, unruly words.

Why am I not allowed to show my strength?

Not show off my cherry lips?

Hide behind my mother's saree?

It is depressing to see how 'feminism'

Is used as a tool to show fake concern;

When their mind thinks of it as nothing more than pocket-sized.

All that I feel is it being thrown and shattered,

Just like our innocence.

When boys, these boys,

They play with our sanity.

The world could be a better place if these boys,

Used their mind and hands,

On things far from women.

If these boys valued the one curve in our bodies,

That is truly alluring, our smile,

Also snatched away.

Now even the touch of a hand for comfort feels empty.

The nights become longer and darker by the minute,

Though this place shines bright pink all the time.

I call this place home.

Not because I'm safest here, but because I have nowhere else to go.

Here destiny makes me realize, each day,

The importance of women in our country.

Watching men walk in and out each day,

Exploiting each one of my kind.

Until, it's my turn.

The larger one preys on the smallest,

I had been taught.

Because that is how the ecosystem works, right?

The hand that wipes my continuous flow of tears,

Sends a shiver down my spine.

Strange, isn't it?

Being afraid of consolance?

Well, my ruined mind did not recognize it anymore.

All children grow up playing with toys,

I grew up with my own share,

Just shaped differently.

All children are taught certain morals,

I had my own share,

Just said differently.

And all of them strive towards a bright future,

I was pushed towards mine,

And it did turn out to be bright,

Bright red.

Photo Credit: Grace Fu

Anticipating

I'm still waiting for the autumn to become yellow.

The time when the leaves and flowers come to life in spring.

The time when the cherry blossoms, bring life to the earth.

The time when it's happy.

I'm still waiting for the child in my neighbor's house to be born.

To hear his laughter echo in the air.

To buy him gifts just so that his tiny tender fingers would hold mine.

So that his innocent eyes light up with joy.

I'm still waiting for the girl I meet at the park, every day, to stop crying.

She wants to kill the boy for cheating on her.

I wonder if she'd ever understand boys.

Or that they aren't worth her tears.

Even her love couldn't make him stay, what profit will the tears do.

I'm still waiting for my maid's daughter to go to school.

So that I can give her the joy of reading my old textbooks.

So that one day she can read the poems I write.

She was always a fan of Rabindranath Tagore, she just wanted to be like him.

I'm still waiting for the pot of gold, at the end of the rainbow.

I want it more than ever, especially this time.

I could use a little luck in life.

I'm still waiting for the day, when my brother grows up.

Wanting to see him for the man he has to become.

And before that the naughty boy, who requires his sister to cover up his mistakes.

I'm still waiting for the darkness to pass.

When the light comes, I will see you clearly.

I will understand what the darkness was trying to hide.

I will see for myself the destruction that you are, clear and bare in the daylight.

I will understand that it's the one thing not worth waiting for.

Photo Credit: Anonymous

Rainbow

Red lights, turn blue.

In them I see you.

Far enough from me, far enough to just see.

I want to wipe that tear away,

Because I know that acid is going to hurt me.

But I feel comfort in the pain.

My silent thoughts now scream at me.

All my life I have been fighting because this society,

They categorize happiness.

His love gave me a home.

A cage in which I desired to be trapped.

From the day my earphones got tangled,

In his fingers for the first time,

I knew he had me wrapped around it too.

He was my king.

We built our own little kingdom together.

When suddenly one day, it all went dark.

It felt like a circuit cut.

But what snapped were not any wires,

But the little string of hope,

I was holding onto all this while.

I want to tell them I am proud of who I am.

I want to make this society feel the pain of the slap that I felt.

I am broken, but I lived through it.

I want to yell in their faces through my tears,

And tell them that,

Here's to the story of another queer boy,

Whose pages you tore,

Just before the best part.

Photo Credit: Samiksha Rungta

Detachment

When I left the city,

I knew I'd have to leave him behind too.

He wasn't ever mine to keep,

wasn't ever mine to hold on to.

I knew what we had

was a love too strong,

for the universe to contain its power.

It was almost not fathomable.

For him, for me.

I knew it when I got myself into this.

Every minute I felt like if I broke into a million pieces today,

every piece will love him.

Love him with the same unconditional feeling that I felt at first.

But it's what will break me,

because I know it's far long gone.

The million pieces

have been writing me poetry to convince me.

Every day, they scream in my ear before I sleep.

Even sleep sends me hints,

when I wake up in the middle of the night,

covered in sweat breathing heavily.

I knew it will kill me as much as

it made me feel alive with energy at the same time.

But we all risk our lives a little, sometime.

It's a different thing that, that's all I did for you.

Ever.

Photo Credit: Dipesh Kundnani

Euphoria

I want to be so deeply in love with someone

that if I walk around the room naked,

he'd smile at me because he thinks I'm beautiful.

I want to be so madly in love

that when he sees the stretch marks on my body,

he thinks that they are just beautiful etchings that have a story
to tell.

I want to be so crazily in love

that when I make chocolate chip pancakes,

he eats it with the most content expression on his face,

even the burnt chocolate.

I want to be so deeply in love

that when it's pouring outside,

I think of dancing in the rain with him,

instead of writing poetry about what the showers took away
with them.

I want to be so crazily in love

that when he looks at me,

he thinks to himself,

"Damn, that's the best thing that could happen to me."

I want to be so madly in love

that when he sees my wrists,

he kisses my scars because he thinks it will lessen the pain.

I want to be so deeply in love

that when someone else looks at us,

they wish for a love like ours.

I want to be so madly in love,

just so that I stop questioning the existence of such a love.

Photo Credit: Grace Fu

Confessed Feelings

Dear long-distance lover,

Yesterday, I dreamt of a date at the best sushi restaurant in town.

It was you, me and a very beautiful pastel pink vanilla scented candle.

The waiter almost dropped the soy sauce

on the new shirt that, I had gifted you just last week, on our one-year anniversary.

As usual, I stopped you from creating a scene,

more like my eyes stopped you.

At work, the girl on the desk next to mine was crying uncontrollably,

because she broke up with her boyfriend.

I consoled her for very long, while I silently prayed

that I don't ever have to see this day.

I know you don't like the color green.

Today, I just could not help but buy the emerald green poster

in the thrift shop, near my apartment that said,

Make peace, not babies. So much like you.

I didn't know what to buy for Jack's wedding present.

I missed you.

I wrote a letter to you, few days ago.

I described everything I had to tell you for all those days that we didn't talk.

I put a print of my red lipstick, the one you really like, at the end of the letter.

The last line I wrote was what I've been wanting to tell you for very long,

'Are we finally ever going to meet?'

-Imagination

Photo Credit: Anonymous

Beauty

Only if time could hold still, just for a bit,

I'd smile to myself just a little longer than usual.

In a world where time zones don't match,

I wish for every moment to somehow be on playback

till I have to inevitably let it go, for good.

Until then, I wish drives would last longer,

only for the reason that the road just won't end.

I wish the rain came more often,

so that we would sit with the windows open with a cup of chai.

I wish for more sleepovers and the endless games of 'dark room'.

I'd wish for everyone to be together, in different time zones.

For all those times to come back,

when World Cup matches were just an excuse

to hang out together beyond curfew.

I'd wish for a standstill right before we all decided to move ahead our way.

To the ones who I went out with for ice cream at 2 in the night,

only because we had done the same for Maggi too many times already.

Somewhere on the path of catching up with life,

and all the stress it throws our way,

I fear we will stop being each other's first birthday wish.

Quite an over-thinker, right?

Photo Credit: Dipesh Kundnani

Is It Really Over?

Late night conversations, life discussions.

I think we spent every last moment in peace.

When you begin to realize that

you are not just living with a bunch of teenagers,

you are actually growing with them,

you begin to see the little things, how they grew on you.

Till today when I call mom, I tell her I miss her,

only because I heard my friend do it each time she called home.

I still think that some detergent is better than the other,

only because someone else thought so too.

Before buying clothes,

I still think it important to ask how the outfit would look on me,

even though she wasn't even physically present in front of me.

I know she would know.

Sending birthday gifts still feels incomplete,

without a birthday card sent alongside, a handwritten one.

A video message for anything big that has happened

in anyone's life seems way more genuine,

than a 'Congratulations' or 'I'm sorry to hear that'.

College being a completely new segment of life,

takes me back to these minute details that make up most of my life.

When I get scars on my body from mistakes that I make,

no one will be there to pick me up and tell me that it is alright.

I want to reminisce these memories till an extent,

where I feel like I'm living in them.

I want them to consume me, whole and soul.

Because I know that if not for this,

never will I ever feel this close to these beautiful beings more than this.

And I do not know any other way to remain sane.

Photo Credit: Samiksha Rungta

It Is Too Much?

There's one minute where all my emotions are exploding

into tiny particles of happiness and,

then there's another where,

I want to break every single thing around me.

My heart cannot take the pressure of the feelings that I feel around you.

It feels lost in a flood in which has no definite way to flow.

I see pictures and quotes about this nonsense,

yet my heart sends them to you and functions as per your response.

It trusts the power you have on it,

Yet it bleeds while questioning it at the same time.

It turns black when you want it to; it becomes gold when you want it.

It feels as though you are its identity, but

it cries because it doesn't know who it is anymore.

My heart feels heavy at the thought of you, but at the same time it's feels safe.

I do not know how it gathers the strength to deal with this,

but turns out it's still working fine.

I tried understanding, put the pieces together each time you shattered them,

only to realize that I use you only to fix them as well.

My heart is so bound by you and everything you do,

it knows nothing else.

You make it smile, you make it cry, you make it heal, yet you break it.

My heart feels like it's caught up in this roller coaster

that doesn't know where it's heading.

One mistake and it will all go tumbling downwards.

Is that going to be the end of this?

Is that going to be the end of the one thing my heart was living off?

How will I expect it to live any further then?

Photo Credit: Dipesh Kundnani

Bare Honesty

I feel like I'm dying.

I've never felt this way before.

I mean it's pretty strange; my insides are crushing me,

And not in the sense that I may feel pain,

But just in the sense that I feel hollow on the inside, as though

I have nothing beneath the skin, no feelings nothing.

I feel like there is something there that's causing me to suffocate

from the inside, but I cannot see what it is,

it's almost like it's black and too out of my vision.

I hate my depression. It keeps taking a toll on me.

I feel like my insides don't exist anymore.

It's almost like a hollow empty feeling.

I keep repeating things. I know it's not the best thing to do.

I just want someone to hear me.

I know that's not the best thing either.

I don't understand the logic behind my body reacting this way

to instances that shouldn't matter to me at such a huge level.

I need to understand my own psyche,

before trying to analyze someone else's.

I know I don't do justice to my happiness, but do my feelings
ever let me?

They take over me in a way that I'm blinded,

and somehow the first thing that I stop seeing is my happiness.

I don't understand how something so small

can have such a huge effect on you.

It makes me angry because why do I give it that much power

that it can hold me against my own self.

I want to face it, scream at it and tell them that they cannot do
anything to me.

I am immune to their silly games and cunning methods.

But the minute they appear in front of me, I feel as though my
knees begin to shake.

I feel as though I choke on my own breath, as though I can taste
blood.

I begin to shiver, my body and my voice.

Then suddenly, I scream really loudly,

no one around me hears it.

And then everything goes pitch black, I feel the cold floor under
me.

No one around me notices.

Photo Credit: Anonymous

Tranquility

She feels like spring on a sultry afternoon.

The kinds where you want to sit in a park bench,

all alone and reminisce the little doings of your life, which have gotten you to this bench.

There's a spark about her that lights up,

each time it lights up, as hope in your heart.

My poems written on the edges of my notebook,

know her so well that when she touches the first page,

all of them come alive.

The colors of the rainbow envy her.

She's a colossal mix of hues that is so difficult to go unnoticed.

The flowers that fall from cherry blossoms come alive, when they touch her skin.

The little doodles on the back of my old school notebooks,

hold traces of her innocence.

The ink in the pens know exactly how she held them,

and the amount of pressure she applied just to get the shape of that heart right, in the center of which she wrote my name.

The sand in the park next to my house, has her footprints imprinted on them.

They know how she skipped her steps, when she walked,

because she knew how important it was to remain happy,

much more than forgetting the importance of that feeling.

She loved eating street food, as much as those vendors loved having her around.

She made them so happy because for her they were not street vendors,

they were just another couple of human beings,

whose life she thought she could brighten up,

just by giving them a smile, each time she saw them.

She smiled so much that she forgot

what it felt like to embrace her fears, her sadness.

She was so lost in making everyone so happy, hers expired.

She did not know what it felt like to face lowly feelings when they hit her.

They became so alien to her, she began to become alien to us, eventually.

For once, when she decided to face the dilemma of her repressed feelings,

was the last time she could be seen.

Photo Credit: Grace Fu

Are You Talking To Me?

I had a dream a few days ago.

I became a detective of sorts.

It was a new strange role.

I was so very used to seeing the sad,

lowly me in every dream that it almost had begun to feel like reality.

I witnessed a murder case.

I didn't have to do much, I just had to solve it.

There was this girl and there was this situation.

She knew she was living, she didn't believe it though.

The minute I made her believe so,

she died.

Did I save her, did I kill her?

How was I supposed to solve that?

I saw the look on her face when she told me about herself.

She said she saw in the color blue,

felt in the color black and

lived in the color purple.

I thought it was a puzzle and if I solved that,

I'd solve her.

She smiled when tears welled up in her eyes.

She told me she felt warm when her skin bled,

right next to her veins on her left wrist,

just a few millimeters from it.

She had a book she read; she was the author of it.

She wrote in it when she felt she couldn't move anymore and

she cried in it when she felt too much.

That book was an open entry straight into her vulnerability.

The day she died when I told her she was living,

I saw it flash in front of her eyes.

She was telling me to open my eyes to what was lying in front
of me.

She was telling me that I could solve this

only if I opened my vision.

I woke up, looked in the mirror,

and told me to open my eyes.

Photo Credit: Dipesh Kundnani

If I Love You

If I love you, I will tell you each day that I do.

I will repeat it till the time your ears feel it's etched inside them.

I will make pancakes for you in the mornings,

when I am satisfied with my workout.

The rest of the days

the cranky me will expect you to wake me up,

with coffee and kisses in bed.

I will drive you to work on the days

when the weather outside coaxes me to come embrace its air.

If I love you, I will send you a rose with your lunchbox,

so that you know,

I was wishing we were having lunch together.

If I told you, I missed you,

I would want you to send me a silly video of you

attempting to send me a flying kiss and failing miserably.

If I love you, I will never be someone else, but myself in front of you.

I will give you more than just my body and skin.

I will give you the thoughts beneath them.

I will show you what it feels like

to make love to someone's feelings.

I would crave for your attention 25 hours in a day,

but trouble you for the same only for about 15.

I will listen to you,

when you crib to me about your boss,

with the third drink of whiskey in your hand.

I will make another one for you and tell you that it's going to be alright.

I will help you grow as a person because that will help me grow too.

If I love you, my soul will love you.

I will never let you feel as though

you are alone in this world.

I will give you all that you could ask for and more.

If I love you, it will be a love that you won't forget.

Photo Credit: Vedant Jain

I Should Have Known

When you left, I didn't cry.

I sat in the prayer room and yelled.

Not because you left,

but because I was alone in this world now.

I screamed at the walls,

I screamed at the air,

I screamed at myself.

My body became half its size.

I guess alcohol and marijuana wasn't fuel enough for it.

Mother made my favorite Mac and cheese.

I had a few bites, I puked.

My body had become used to the hollow empty feeling.

It had fallen in love with it.

The minute I let something invade it, it threw it out.

When you left,

the lights in my street began to burn dimmer.

They began to show me that it wasn't safe outside anymore.

When you left, I knew.

I had to finally use the alarm clock that you had bought me ages ago.

I unpacked it.

The next minute it was in a trillion pieces on the floor.

Dad was getting worried about me.

He said I would go crazy if I didn't stop behaving the way I was.

How could I explain to him that a whole part of me was missing?

The part that kept me sane,

without which I became what I was that day.

When you left the air smelled different.

It smelled of the burnt toast in the neighbor's house and of the dead fish in our fish tank.

I loved gifts, you know I did.

I throw them right in the garbage when I get them now.

The garbage guy thanks me every day till today for the scarf Annie gave me,

which he went and gave his sister.

You used to tell me to socialize less.

I gave those people a home in my thoughts when I met them.

They laugh at me now.

It's miserable.

When you left, my happiness left with you.

I didn't know how empty one's soul can feel,

even though it is just one person, who has walked out of their heart.

Photo Credit: Dipesh Kundnani

IS THIS LIVING?

I am living, I am breathing.

The night is starry.

The ball of gases talk to me.

Their twinkling is a language,

something like the morse code.

They tell me that I'm alive.

I tell them I want to die.

But I don't know.

Does the camaraderie of the two,

feel what living feels like?

I don't know if the flowers in my garden,

still bloom as bright as they used to.

The sun shines brighter,

my vision goes dimmer.

The air around me becomes choking.

But I don't know.

Is this what living feels like?

Dead and ignited at the same time.

I hold your fingers in my hand.

They slip out of mine just as quickly.

I want to hold them longer.

My hands are forgetting,

the familiarity of their touch.

My body is slowly losing its senses,

all five of them.

But I don't know.

I want to dress up,

put on my favorite lipstick,

and go dancing under neon lights.

The stranger has his arms on my body,

the touch is not new.

But I don't know.

Is that what living feels like?

The unfamiliarity of things becoming familiar.

But I don't know.

Will I ever?

Photo Credit: Dipesh Kundnani

II. SO LITTLE YET SO MUCH

Bliss

The fighting mother

made her last wish for a tub of ice cream.

That night the hospital room saw,

the happiest a family had ever been in it.

Photo Credit: Vedant Jain

Minutiae

Once upon a time,

teardrops rested on their tips.

Today replaced by raindrops,

I fell in love with her eyelashes.

Photo Credit: Grace Fu

Yearning

The night stars

don't feel like them anymore.

But this time,

I hope I don't miss that shooting star.

Photo Credit: Grace Fu

Fondness

I talk to him,

and my period cramps go away.

That's the kind of love,

you should aspire to chase.

Photo Credit: Anonymous

Charade

The kajal in his eyes, the black pathani.

The muslin cloth around his head.

At the age of 10 he was told,

It was just a fancy dress competition.

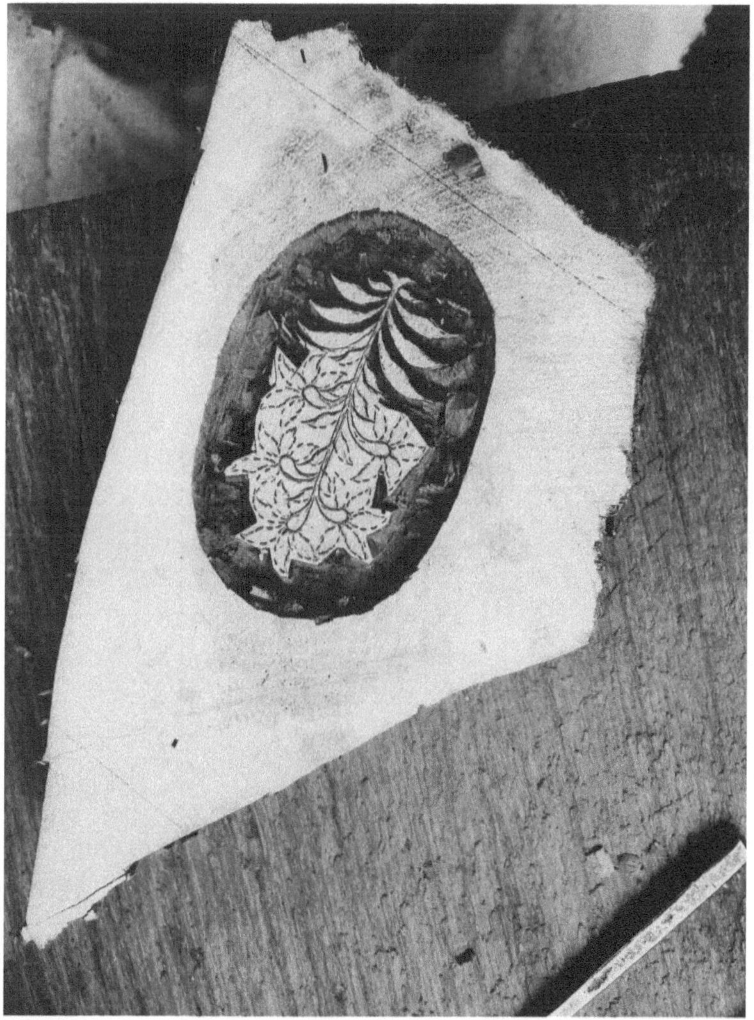

Photo Credit: Vedant Jain

Remembrance

The vanilla scented candles,

Just took me back to that Italian bar,

The night of September 14th.

I didn't know a mere candle march held for you,

Had the strength to create illusions.

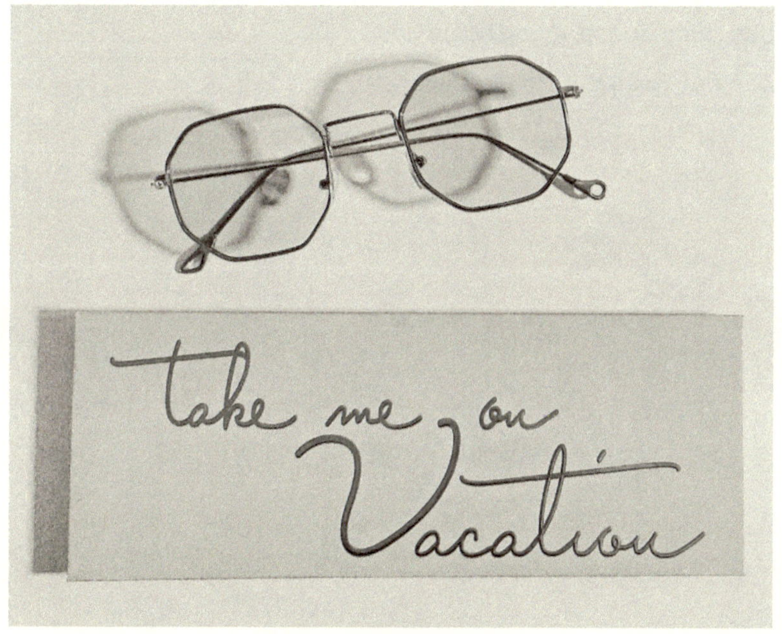

Photo Credit: Anonymous

Home

She said she was going home.

She ran straight into his arms.

Photo Credit: Grace Fu

Usual

I came home to

Freshly baked cookies.

The house didn't smell

like blood for once.

Photo Credit: Vedant Jain

Alien

The first time our eyes met,

I thought you were different.

A few days later

When I saw you in the bar,

I realized you had grown up.

Photo Credit: Dipesh Kundnani

Admiration

Lying naked, spent.

I could only think of how

Your love cost nothing

But a smile and a click.

Photo Credit: Anonymous

Triumph

The blush covering the bruise,

Was slowly dripping down her cheeks.

She wiped away her happy tears,

As the accused were sentenced to death.

Photo Credit: Grace Fu

Astonishing

She looked at him with eager eyes,

As he hid the ring behind his back.

'Almost there', he motivated himself,

Eyes shut.

He couldn't understand the drips,

The monitored heartbeat,

The next time he opened them.

Photo Credit: Vedant Jain

Concern

Hari colored the shade of unicorns,

A perpetual smile plastered on her face.

One day I noticed her,

Wipe her tears through the same broken smile.

And I remember my eyes wondering,

Which outnumbered which;

The number of colors in her hair,

Or the number of slits on her wrist.

Photo Credit: Anonymous

Intimacy

What makes me, me and what makes you, you?

Is that you still love your old Bourbon,

And I'm still hooked to

My newly bought chardonnay.

What makes me, me and what makes you, you

Is that you told me yesterday that you wanted a cat,

And I had just cried to you about my dog dying.

But what makes us, us

Is that we still think it's cute to kiss

When our cart reaches the top of the ferris wheel.

Photo Credit: Samiksha Rungta

www.ingramcontent.com/pod-product-compliance
Lightning Source LLC
La Vergne TN
LVHW040014200726
843493LV00005B/1261